I AM

The Key to Manifesting

Vivian Amis

I Am – The Key to Manifesting

Copyright © 2015 by Vivian Amis

ISBN: 978-0-9749326-5-1

Printed in United States of America

DEDICATION

To the world's inhabitants,

May this book guide you
toward enlightenment and
toward the fulfillment and
manifestation of a truly
deserved life of Love,
Peace and Joy...

CONTENTS

Introduction

There are thousands of books on the market in regards to manifestation and creating a happy life. So, why another book?

From my perspective, many people are still not using the knowledge they currently have to create the life they desire to experience and to eliminate suffering.

This may be due to the fact that there is a lack of belief, which is a vital key in creation, but maybe there is simply a misunderstanding of the principle which makes all things happen.

This book is an attempt to help build faith through sharing some of my own personal experiences and to clarify some misunderstandings in hope of building a solid foundation of understanding who you truly are so you too may create a better life for yourself and for those around you.

Who Am I?

If you have a hard time believing in a Genie in the sky that will grant you every wish.....rightfully so.

If you have a hard time believing that there is a law outside of you that pulls all things you desire towards you....rightfully so.

If you were not successful at manifesting the things you desire in your life using a Genie or a law outside of you, then it's not because you did something wrong. In order for anything to manifest in your life, good or bad, you have to first believe in the possibility. There is no Genie in the sky nor any law outside of you. Nothing is outside of YOU. All power is within YOU. You are the creator of your experience.

So, who are you?

When you were born, you were a clean slate. You were without beliefs and thoughts, but then something happened. You noticed a person outside of you. You did not understand why there were "others" and the question "Who am I" was born and would continue to be the driving force in all your searches, throughout your life. You perceived things through your senses: you heard sounds through your ears, saw things through your eyes, you felt hunger, cold, warmth and touch. You tasted food through your taste organs and recognized your mother's smell through your nose. If you cried or laughed, people would react a certain way. When you pooped in your diaper, the person changing you probably made a face.

You learned something from all these things and put them into categories of good and bad based on the how they made you feel and how others around you reacted.

Even though the search for who you are continued throughout your life, it has changed to many things. This is due to the fact that you believed what others told you what you were seeking, not truly knowing what they were seeking themselves. So, you sought success believing that would bring you happiness, you sought a partner believing that would bring you happiness, and you sought the perfect body believing that would bring you happiness. Because somehow deep down you knew that whatever you were truly seeking would bring you happiness.

The problem is that you forgot what you were seeking and searched in the world hoping to find "it" there, while all along covering up more and more of who you truly are even before all these things appeared to you and became a part of who you think you are.

I too found myself seeking at one point. I read every self-help book I could get my hands on. I had learned quite fast that it was not something in this physical realm and dove deeper and deeper into metaphysics and esoteric.

There are different vehicles such as meditation, prayer, yoga or contemplation to realize your true Self, but no matter what the vehicle is that you use, you have to realize it yourself in order for this to become your experience. A master may show you the vehicle he used to realize his Self, but no Master can do it for you.

For me it was contemplation: One day while sitting outside on my back porch, I thought about God and where God is when I heard: *I am closer than you think.*

My first reaction was, of course, *everyone knows that.* God is wherever I am, but I heard nothing in reply. Instead there was this silence, you know, the one where two people are talking and one doesn't reply so you add something to get a response.

So I thought about the statement: *Closer than you think.* Closer than thinking, thinking, thought, closer than thought, before thought! I got it. A light bulb went off ....Before thought there is silence in my mind and I found God and my true Self in that silence.

In the silence of our minds, we are one with God. Only in the silence of our minds are we One. One with all.

There is no separation, no differences, no judgment.....we are all the same in the silence of our minds. In the silence of our minds, which is simply the absence of thought, we are in the pure state of being and from the state of being we can be anything.

We are Gods creating our own worlds individually as well as collectively through our being. Our being is *I am* and it does not matter if we are conscious about it or not.

Everyone is being something or someone. There is no one who is not.

"I am" is the foundation that all else is created upon. It is your awareness that you exist.

Ever since you were born into this physical realm, what you think and call "you" has changed. Your body has changed from being a baby to being a child to being an adult. Your hair has changed, and you may have even changed your name.

You have changed what you do from just lying there in a crib to learning in school to working a job and went from being a baby to being a child and being an adult. You may now have a title, have children, and you may now be the owner of a car, a house or a business.

All your life everything about "you" has changed and is still subject to change, but there is one thing that will never change and that is YOU. The real YOU.

You being...I am. You have always existed. You existed before you became anything in particular. And that is who you truly are.

Realizing the real Self means a going back to, not a becoming. That is why so many seek but do not find. They have a hard time realizing their true Self, because they think they have to do something in order to be. They think: If I do this, then I will be, or if I do that, then I will be. But you "are" already that which you are seeking. In other words, you are not a person, a mother, a Doctor...you are the "I am" before you became anything in particular.

You cannot know your true Self in terms of knowledge, as all knowledge is within and of the mind.

The true Self is closer than mind, therefore you have to be "out of your mind" to realize your true Self.

Once everything the mind thinks you are is dismissed, all knowledge and beliefs are removed and you know nothing; the Self is revealed.

All you can truly know is that you exist and that is all you know in the absence of all knowledge, concepts, beliefs and thought. You don't know what you are, but you know that you are. This is the real Self. It is knowing the real Self in the absence of knowledge, as all knowledge is in and of the mind.

The only way to know the real Self in the absence of knowledge is to be "it".

Being "it" you are One with that and you are that. There are no two: you and who you think you are. There is only YOU.

Beliefs

Beliefs are programs. These programs run constantly and are creating your experience. Imagine your mind being a computer. What you perceive through your senses is the information you enter into the computer. If the mind recognizes a pattern, it creates a belief. These beliefs are not based on the truth. No belief is, but there are some beliefs that may serve you as you walk in the physical realm of things.

From an idea, which was just a possibility that you opened up to, you locked your mind into that possibility and then searched unconsciously for the validation of that new "truth" and ended up with a belief that soon would manifest into something physical that you then experienced.

Some beliefs serve you as you walk this physical plain, but others do not.

If you recognize a pattern in your experiences, then you have a belief that is running your life. If it is a good pattern, keep the belief, but if it is a belief that does not serve you, you have the choice to break that belief.

Scientists are finding that thoughts are things. Thoughts are matter. Matter is energy. Nothing really matters in the physical realm but through our belief in something we create the illusion of that thing.

The whole material/physical world is said to be an illusion and what that means is that matter underneath a microscope is nothing but molecules moving around and blinking in and out of existence. The reason these particles blink in and out of existence is because we are creating them in an instant.

One day I was watching an airplane fly across the sky, and I thought: Did God create this airplane or did man? Does Spirit need an airplane to travel from one place to another? We believe we are or have a body and this body needs to go with us wherever we go, so we come up with ideas on how to create a vessel in which the body can be moved, such as cars, bikes, boats, airplanes and so on.

We created chairs to sit on and beds to lie in because we believe our body needs to rest.

And we create food and drinks because we believe that our body needs to eat and drink.

God is a Spirit and we were made in "his" likeness and image, so we too must be a spirit. Spirit does not have a physical body, nor does it know of any needs such as to sit, to travel, to rest or to eat.

A few Masters have demonstrated that the body can live without food and drink. These Masters have overcome the physical realm by removing the belief that they are their body.

There is no judgment on eating or drinking or having this belief. It actually serves a purpose in our society.

The point I am trying to make here is that it is a belief that you are the body and that you need food and drink to maintain the body.

Life Is Fair

I am sure you have heard the question "Why do bad things happen to good people?", but bad things happen to both good people and bad people equally. Good things happen to happy people.

Someone very wise once said many years ago: "God shines his light on the just and on the unjust equally." There is no God that rewards or punishes anyone. There is no God that gives or takes away anything. That is why so many prayers go unanswered.

You are the creator of your experiences. God created the bigger picture which is harmonious and perfect and you as an individual paint in the details, which are sometimes not so pleasant.

God in this sense, is that part of you that is real and unchanging…the real YOU. There is no God outside of you, but as we live in the physical realm of things, God appears to be divided into many parts: animals, plants, trees and humans. God is Life. There are many lives and forms of living but only one life, and we are all part of that life. This life is *I am*, in many different shapes and forms, but in essence the same.

Through your state of being, by being something in particular you create your experiences.

Whatever follows the "I am" is who you are being in particular: I am a Mother, I am a child, I am rich, I am overweight and so on.

The outside appearance of things is created through your belief in that possibility. By the 'outside', I mean everything from your thoughts to your relationships to the world as you see it and experience it.

You get what you believe to be true. You experience what you believe to be true about any subject. You create from the inside out and the world will always reflect back to you your beliefs about it. Seeing is not believing but the other way around: Believing is seeing.

Life gives you what you create...not what you deserve. This may seem unfair at first sight and the question arises: why do "bad" people get away with "bad" things? But no one is really getting away with anything.

You can lie to those around you, but you cannot deceive your true Self.

When I was little, my mother used to say that God sees everything when I tried to get away with something. Today I understand that there is no God sitting on a cloud judging me as good or bad; we are the greatest judge upon ourselves, which is reflected through our very own feelings of guilt or shame. No matter how hard we try to dismiss or ignore these feelings, they are there.

We know right from wrong not based on what our parents have taught us but based on the feeling certain actions create within us.

Going back to the bigger picture, to the truth of who you are, you could be experiencing bliss and that bliss would be a good indicator that you are on the right track, and that your thoughts and actions are in harmony with each other.

Since you are the creator of your experience, when you have feelings of shame and guilt, you will create more circumstances that will create more feelings of shame and guilt.

There is no law outside of you that will come back at you and punish you.

YOU are the one that punishes yourself by creating over and over again circumstances that make you feel bad. That is why it is said to come as you are. Give up the past and start over. Yesterday is yesterday and long gone.

Today is a new day and for that matter this moment is a brand new moment. In this very moment you can change your future simply by becoming silent and realizing your true Self....beyond mind.

The
Three Aspects of Life

There are 3 areas in your life that you will want to be aware of in order to have a truly fulfilled life. If one of these areas is not aligned with the desire you would like to experience, the loss will spill over and affect other areas of your life as well.

The areas are as follows:

<u>Love:</u> This area covers all your relationships with yourself and with others, how people react to you and how they treat you. Relationships also include teachers, parents, friends, children, siblings, partner, co-workers, business partners and neighbors.

Even though you may not realize it, your very being is Love. The physical love we seek from others is the closest we can get to "the real thing". The downside to seeking love from others is that the love of this world is conditioned and limited to only a few people in your life.

If you knew yourself to be Love, no one could add or subtract Love from you. You would not experience suffering if someone withdrew "love" from you and no one could take advantage of you. Knowing your true Self as Love, your cup would be full to the brim and running over and you would share simply with others from the spill.

This Love that you truly are is unconditional. It is not conditioned to someone deserving your love, and it can never be held back from anyone.

You being Love you bless everyone you meet, you have compassion with all, not just the victim but also the victimizer.

Joy: This area covers your physical things such as your body, your money, your job and your belongings. When I say money, I don't just mean how much you make but also how much money you actually have to fulfil your needs and wants. If you focus on the money you make alone, then you may make a lot of money but there will be things that happen to you or to those around you that will "eat" your money, leaving you without enough money.

This is a trap a lot of people fall into to. People think they need to make more money and strive for raises and promotions believing that they then will have more money.

Not so, they will only make more money. Big difference!

If your bills or what goes out is higher than what comes in, you are not richer. What gives you the feeling and brings about the experience of having more money is the actual money you have left to do whatever you please with.

This may be saving, or going on a vacation or spoiling yourself or someone else with a shopping spree. It is the "extra" money left over after all "needs" are met.

That is what you want. You want to have choices.

Your job or what you do for a living can be a source through which your joy flows.

If you hate your job or get no fulfillment out of your job, you will have no motivation to go to work and you will use every excuse not to go. You can find purpose in almost every job, if you look for it. Money is never a motivator even if it looks that way, and maybe it was the first initial purpose for why you went to work, but after time sets in, you will lose interest in your job, no matter how much money you make.

If you are not satisfied with your body, your weight and your health, then no matter how much money you make, you will be unhappy. All the money in the world will not matter if you can't enjoy it and participate in life the way you deserve it.

Being ill or not satisfied with your body will limit you in how you experience life as it is meant to be experienced and life as it could be experienced.

As humans we seek joy in material things which include the body. Happiness is the closest we can get to the "real thing". But happiness is temporary and dependent on you having something; if you lose it or don't get that something you are unhappy.

Joy is simply being aware that you exist. It is an excitement for life itself and whatever comes your way. It is the innocence of a child and looking through a child's eyes as if life were an adventure, and every day, every moment being a new beginning.

Peace: This area relates to your mind and covers your emotions, your beliefs, your attachments, your thoughts and your state of mind all together. If you are depressed, anxious, fearful, or have compulsive thoughts that are bombarding you, then what good is all the wealth and health if you can't enjoy it?

The mind is a mysterious thing. If I had to answer the question "What is mind?", I would say it is an instrument through which we perceive and translate what we perceive into concepts. Through the mind we learn and retain experiences.

The problem with mind and why you experience suffering is that you believe you are your mind. The mind is neither good nor bad, it is the oneness with mind that creates pleasure or suffering depending on the thoughts we give our attention to and become one with.

Peace is when the mind is at rest. In the absence of thought there is silence. This silence is not nothingness but a no thing. The mind is not thinking of anything. It is not worrying about tomorrow but living in the moment that is presented to you right now.

One way to quiet the mind is to meditate on a daily basis. In meditation you learn to control your mind by teaching it to focus on one thing only. First the mind will rebel like a little child that has never learned to listen, but with time the thoughts will slow down and the mind will become quiet when needed.

When your attention goes into the past or into the future, you move away from the present, the present of this moment and all future moments.

The past is dead and holds resentment. The future is unborn and holds fear. The only time that truly exists and is alive is this very moment.

Keep this moment alive but stay focused only on that which is happening right now. Right now you are reading...

Feelings vs Emotions

The difference between feelings and emotions is that feelings are divine. Feelings have nothing to do with anything happening outside of you.

Emotions are reactions to outer circumstances.

By outer circumstances I mean things that you experience through your belief in duality: good and bad.

Example:

Someone gives you a compliment – you feel good.

Someone rejects your idea – you feel bad.

You have the perfect weight – you feel good.

You are overweight – you feel bad.

Your partner brings you flowers – you feel good.

Your partner forgets your birthday – you feel bad.

Emotions are just that. Emotions are not divine, there are reactions. When you react, you are responding to a belief in a separation. There is no you, me and God. We are one.

The belief in a separation, which was the first and original lie, set us up for suffering.

There are only three feelings that are divine: Love, Peace and Joy.

They are divine because you can experience them independent from any thought.

And because they are divine, you do not need an outside source to experience them and they are present without a reason or cause.

When you have realized your true Self, you come to understand that Love, Peace and Joy are the very aspects of YOU and the search is over.

When all three feelings come together and your life is aligned with the truth of who you truly are, then you experience bliss and you realize that you are that bliss and that Love, Peace and Joy are just an aspect of your divine Self.

Keys to Manifesting

Even though the search may be over, the question arises: What am I going to do now?

Now you have fun. Now you start changing the physical...consciously.

The key to manifesting anything in your life is to <u>be</u> what you want to experience. The secret here is to know that whatever you believe to <u>be</u> will reflect outwards as an appearance.

As you "are" being creates the outside and will validate that belief back to you. And yes you are….. fill in the blanks.

You may have heard that this world is Maya…an illusion. What is meant by that is the world outside of us is to our own making; it is changeable.

We change the world when we change our being from one thing to another: I am this or I am that.

Therefore the outside is nothing but the inside reflected outwards. They are one and the same. The outside is to the inside like the sun's ray is to the sun. One does not appear without the other.

As you are, so you have. Being and having are one. You are…you have. What you have is simply that which is directly proportionate with who you think you are.

If you believed you were rich, your life and belongings would reflect back to you that which you believe symbolizes the life of a rich person.

Now that may be different for each one of us, but you get the picture. If you believed you were poor, you would not have enough money to pay your bills or buy the things you need.

When you realize that you have the power and are that power, you can create whatever it is that you would like to experience. Turn away from the outside; stop trying to change the outside. Go to the source within your mind that created the appearance.

All problems must be met within your own mind, within your own belief.

Once the belief is changed or removed, the outside will change and that problem will be removed.

The way to change the outside is to look within you for the belief of being that is creating the appearance.

As you believe, so be it done

The Realm
of All Possibilities

In order to open your mind further to the possibilities of state of being, let's talk about Consciousness. Consciousness is the field of all possibilities. The field of all possibilities includes possibilities that you are aware of and unaware of. Possibilities are ideas. Someone that has an idea opens himself or herself up to that possibility. That is how world records are broken. Someone has an idea that was never done before and opens his or her mind to that possibility and once he or she achieves it, others follow shortly after.

This is an important factor in creating a life of your desires, because if you have so far only chosen from that which you think is possible, you are limiting yourself from experiencing the magnificence of YOU.

When you choose only from what you know, you will never experience anything different and will continue to create the same thing.

When a thought comes into your mind, be aware of it and don't let your mind lock itself into that possibility.

Especially if it is one that you don't want to experience.

What you choose to believe becomes your experience, and the whole goal of creating consciously is that you want to experience whatever it is that you want to have or be.

The "I am" of you being conscious of your real Self, also referred to as being the light of the world, is that which makes all things appear.

Pure state of being is not conscious about being anything in particular but, for the purpose of manifesting, we need to step into the field of consciousness and choose consciously that which we would like to experience and align our state of being with that possibility.

The statement that all things are possible to God means that in the state of "I am" you can create anything in the physical realm of things. In this state of pure being or field of all possibilities, you can choose consciously to change your life, change your experience and manifest whatever it is you desire.

It is like going to a store full of all things before they are manifested into things. They are possibilities and ideas. You choose from this field of possibilities, through your belief of who you are, which then in turn becomes your experience and manifests.

One day my husband and I were on our way to the bank to deposit a check, and we stopped at a store on our way to pick up some groceries. While we were still in the store, we tried to get money from the ATM machine located inside of the store, but my ATM card was declined. Immediately my mind started asking questions as to why my card was declined. I originally thought I still had money on my account, but now I was not sure anymore. I thought about payments that could have gone through that

I may have forgotten to subtract or maybe someone stole my card number and used it. Then I remembered that I was picking and choosing from the field of all possibilities and said to myself that those were some possibilities, but all things are possible. So I kept my mind free from attaching myself to any one particular idea and outcome.

When we arrived at the bank, I found that I still had funds in my account and that nothing was wrong or missing.

The ATM machine at the store was probably simply defective and did not read my card correctly.

When you are conscious about something, you are picking that possibility from the field of all possibilities. If you lock yourself into a possibility, that possibility becomes your experience.

In the field of all possibilities everything is perfect and harmonious and, when we affirm that all things are possible, we shift our mind away from that which is possible based on our past experiences to a possibility that will be perfect and harmonious.

When confronted with a problem, open your mind to finding a solution. Don't assume a negative outcome. You have the power to create your experience and will create your experience based on which possibility your mind locks into, unless you keep your mind open to all possibilities.

The
Power of Attention

Attention is the opening up of the possibility to an idea. No idea is really based on the Truth, but serves a purpose in creating our life and life experiences. The focusing of attention on any idea is the first step in creating your experience.

Attention is the tool through which you choose from the field of all possibilities. Attention is you shining your light upon a possibility. The light brings your ideas or that which you seek to find, consciously or not, good or bad, into your consciousness. You as the witness or observer shine your light (attention) upon the movie screen (consciousness) and are able to watch/perceive anything that happens on the movie screen. The title of the movie is "Your Life".

Whatever you give attention to appears and becomes a part of your consciousness.

Attention is you choosing (consciously or not) from the field of all possibilities. Everyone is choosing right now, but many do not know that it is a choice. They are the victims in life choosing the same misery they experienced in the past because they never opened their mind to any other possibility.

When you are aware that you are not only the creator of your experiences, but that you have a choice to create your life and experiences consciously, with intent and on purpose, then life becomes fun. That does not mean you don't still make mistakes, as old beliefs still linger and have to be pulled by their roots one by one, but it does mean that you will start to change your life and choose consciously what it is that you would like to experience.

Consciously giving your attention to that which you would like to experience is like asking for that which you want. You may have heard the saying: "Ask and you shall receive." Giving attention to something is the asking.

That is why gratitude works. In gratitude you give thanks to that which you have.

By focusing your attention on that which you know you have, you create more of that which you want.

That is why you can start wherever you are. You don't need to be rich, you just need a penny. You don't even need a penny, you could be thankful for the clothes you wear, or the breath you breathe. It is not so much the thing you are thankful for but the feeling of having "something" that brings about you having more.

I remember a time when I experienced lack and a friend told me that she saw me abundant. I asked her, "Where?" and she said, "You have four children. That is abundance." I thought about it and saw the possibility of it. Having four children in today's society is truly a lot.

See, abundance is not just money; abundance simply means a lot of something. After that awareness, I was able to see that I had an abundance of hair and even of bills. The feeling of having a lot took over my whole being and I started to truly feel abundant. I opened my mind to that possibility by putting my attention on the things I did have a lot of.

Creating
the Experience

There are two steps in creating an experience:

1) Know what you want to have

2) Create the feeling of having it now.

Even though the first step seems simple and logical, most people never move into this step. These are the people that are stuck in their realty. They complain, feel sorry for themselves and blame others for their misery.

Misery however serves a purpose. It lets you know what you don't want. In order to know what you want, you need to know what you don't want.

Use misery as your stepping stone, but don't forget to step off of the stone. Take on the responsibility that you are the creator of your experience, which also means that you can change your experience.

Don't try to figure out how things will change, because that is none of your business. Things could change through many different ways and, when you try to figure out the how and why, you limited yourself from the blessing that has not yet been revealed to you.

Everything is moving toward the realization of Self and Oneness; whatever serves this purpose will unfold for the good of all involved.

Your job is simply to move right into the feeling of having it now. That's it.

In order to truly feel you have that which you would like to experience, you have to become one with it. You have to know it with all your heart and you cannot have any doubt.

It cannot be a possibility, but must be that possibility. It's a "locking" of the mind into an agreement of an idea: I am this or that. This "state of being" cannot be based on the idea that you need it or want it. This "state of being" must be based on the idea that it is actually true.

The second step therefore must be that you claim to have the things already that go along with being this or that.

Example: When you can't pay your bills and don't have enough money to buy the things you need...you may consider yourself as poor. Your belief in that case would be: I am poor. You feel poor and everything outside of you reflects back to you and confirms your belief....I am poor...and you are.

In order to create money, you would have to shift the focus of attention from what you don't have to what you do have.

This can be done in different ways.

Visualization

One way to create the experience is to use your imagination to manifest it.

The mind does not differentiate between what is already manifested and what is yet to be manifested. To the mind these things are the same. Visualization can be done with your eyes closed or by looking at a picture.

I used this technique to manifest wooden floors in our house. I searched on the internet for the exact color and style that I wanted and saved the picture as my computer background. Whenever I sat down at my computer, I looked at the picture and imagined me having these floors and what that would feel like.

I sought the feeling within me until I truly felt it, and then went about my way. Within three weeks, we were installing our new wooden floors, bought with money from an unexpected source.

Gratitude

The reason Gratitude works well in manifesting something you would like to experience is because, as you focus your attention on what you do have, you create more of it. This is the nature of who you in truth are.

What you are thankful for becomes a part of your consciousness and now "belongs" to you. It was always yours, but it just wasn't part of your awareness.

That is why those that have will have more, and those that have less, what they have will be taken away. Having goes together with state of being. You cannot separate those two. These two are one. Where there is an inside there too must be an outside.

Who we are being, manifests outside of us the validation of that belief. Therefore we are not only being thankful, we are also having the belongings that go with being thankful.

Exercise: Think of a problem you are experiencing right now in your life. Now look at what you do have in your life that shows a little bit of what you would like more of and give thanks to that.

Your focus of attention must shift from the problem to the solution and give thanks for that.

Crack the belief

This reminds me of a time when I was allergic to the instant glue used for fingernails. I would get my fingernails done and, as my nails are very soft, I added tips. These tips were applied to the real nail with a special glue that is super strong and dries very fast.

Every time this glue was used, my fingers broke out in a rash. It was very annoying, and I had to wear gloves to wash dishes as water seemed to make things worse. I had this problem for many years, until one day at the nail salon, I asked the nail technician if she could use something else to apply the tips. To her question, "Why?", I explained my allergic reaction to the glue. Another nail technician that was walking by stopped to see what the problem was. After explaining to her my allergic reaction and repeating my question about the possibility of using something else to apply the nails, she told me that I didn't have an allergic reaction to the glue, but to the oil used after the nails were applied. She said that she had been a nail technician for many years and had never heard of an allergic reaction to the glue. She was so convincing and there was no doubt in her mind that I actually was thinking of that possibility. It was not a final possibility in my mind as I did not always use the oil, yet still broke out in hives. Yet her belief was strong enough to "crack" my belief.

Once the crack happened, light shone through the lie and I was cured once and for all. I did not however accept her belief as a new belief. I knew for sure that it was not the oil, but it was enough to crack my old belief.

Exercise:

Think of an experience you are encountering right now in this moment, such as: My Boss does not give me any recognition.

Now try to remember a time where you did get recognition from your boss. It may be something very small, such as a pat on your shoulder, or an e-mail, or a smile, or your boss trusted you with an important task. If you look for it, you will find it. It is there, but your belief is building a block through which you cannot see anything other than your belief reflecting back to you. The goal is to prove yourself wrong.

Affirmations

Affirmations are words or sentences spoken repeatedly. Affirmations should always contain the new idea as if it is done.

Example: I am abundant, I am healthy, I am successful

The reason affirmations work is because words we think or speak to our selves, sink into our subconscious minds if we say them often enough and remove current existing beliefs and create a new belief and new patterns of thinking.

Affirmations should be repeated until the new belief is firmly established within the subconscious mind. Only then will these positive statements bring about the desired results.

Exercise: Think of something you would like to experience and form a positive "I am/I have" statement that will reflect what you would like to experience.

I suggest that you try all the different ways on how to create and see what works best for you.

Co-creating
with Others

You may have heard the idea that there are no "others". This idea stems from the truth of oneness and that in truth we are one with all life.

How we co-create our experiences with others is based on two things:

1) Who you believe you are

Who you believe you are reflects outward and others will affirm it back to you.

Example: If you believe you are overweight, others will bring to your attention that you are overweight.

If you believe you are rich, beautiful or wise, others will reflect that back to you and it will be a part of your experience. Instead of getting upset at someone telling you that you are a liar, ask yourself: Where am I lying to myself or do I believe I am a liar? All problems must be met within your own self. Others are only reflecting and telling you what you believe about yourself.

This is not something to get upset about or offended about. It is a blessing. If others would not bring it to your attention, you would continue to choose from the field of possibilities that which does not serve you.

Change who you think you are by choosing consciously who you would like to be, and others will bring that to your attention.

What others see in you or think about you is none of your business. That is between God and them, but what is brought to your attention is between God and you, because it is a part of YOUR consciousness.

Others will appear to you based on:

2) Who you believe they are.

How others appear to you is based on your belief about who you think they are. In the physical appearance of things, people may have the appearance of being this or that.

A true Master sees through the appearance to the truth of who you are.

The Master knows that you are perfect even before you became anything in particular.

If someone appears to you anything other than perfect, you must look within your own beliefs and ask yourself: Do I believe in the possibility that others could be anything other than perfect?

In order to experience someone differently, you have to change the belief you have about who you think they are.

If you believed you had great co-workers, your belief would create that and that would become your experience.

If you believed your children were bad and misbehaved and needed to be disciplined, then that too would be your experience.

Exercise: Think of ten people in your life right now and think about the way they appear to you. Now, choose consciously how you would like to experience each person by changing the focus of your attention away from the problem onto the solution.

You can't change others, but you can change the way you see them, which will in turn change your experience of them.

Becoming the Witness

One day while fighting with my husband, I noticed a "me" inside of me. I know it sounds strange but this other "me" was observing me fighting. As I put my attention on this other "me" I noticed that she was completely at peace. She was watching, lovingly, that which was going on but was completely detached. As I looked around I saw that this "me" was within and connected to all living things yet nothing in particular...it was life itself.

I understood that we are nothing; we can perceive as we are simply that which perceives, we are the witness to the body, to the mind and to that which is happening in the world. I realized that nothing was my true self....I was simply a witness to everything.

You too are not anything your mind can perceive. Everything your mind perceives is an illusion and is subject to change. The real Self is beyond mind and never changes. To go beyond mind, you have to separate your real Self from who you think you are. If you can see your body...you are not your body. You cannot perceive your body and be your body at the same time. Who is seeing the body?

If you can stop your mind from thinking or observe a thought...you are not your mind.

In order to "pop out" you must experience my words, not just read them. You have to separate your true Self from mind. Observe your thought. Not what you are thinking, but observe that experience of your thinking. Grab a hold of one thought and look at it....and realize this truth: That is a thought...it is not good or bad, but simply a thought. Now ask yourself: Who is observing this thought?

As humans, we mistakenly believe we are the body and mind, but we are that which observes the body and mind.

You, as the witness, still observe what is going on around you, but without attachment to the outcome.

You, as the witness, do not judge what is going on around you, but look at it from a bigger picture. It's like looking through God's eyes to what is going on.

In a bigger picture everything is in perfect order and working toward to the realization of oneness. From a limited perspective there may be suffering involved, but from a bigger perspective every experience is a blessing and serves a much greater purpose.

There is only one path....and everyone is on it and there is only one Truth, but many definitions of that truth.

Everything serves a purpose and is serving the same purpose, and everyone is trying their best with the knowledge and understanding they have at any given moment.

As the witness, you are detached from the details because you know that in the end it will be perfect. Whatever the outcome may be.

Living a life of being the witness, it is easy for you to get along with others and move between two worlds. One being the physical world that is observed and one being the world within.

You may still get pulled into the physical realm of things and into believing these things are true. The physical realm feels very real, and it is a great temptation not to get pulled into the appearance of things, but with time and practice, it becomes easier to just stay the witness.

One more clarification is needed to fully grasp this state of being and that is to understand that you are not ignoring anything that is happening around you; it is actually the opposite of that. You realize that you are the creator of your experience and co-create with others. In order to give yourself and the world your highest good, you must become and remain single-eyed and keep your eye on the bigger picture which is harmonious and perfect for all.

Creating as the witness is a little different. The witness acknowledges that which is in front of him, but does not judge according to the appearance of things.

The witness realizes that there are manifestations that may appear to be good or bad but does not react to the appearance. The witness never leaves the real Self that is at peace even though the world may be falling apart around him. The witness never leaves the real Self that is Love, no matter what anyone does to him. The witness never leaves Joy, no matter what is taken from him.

The witness does not create consciously. He has stepped out of the creating process and has become a witness to that which already has been created: Peace, Love and Joy and perfection. He sees the bigger picture and keeps his eyes on the bigger picture.

When a problem is brought to his attention, he takes no thought to the appearance, and miracles happen beyond one's imagination. This is due to the fact the imagination is always limited to what the mind can come up with. The witness does not limit his understanding to imagination but dwells and lives and has his state of being in the unimaginable, which he demonstrates, while not fearing an appearance nor buying into the appearance believing it is true, no matter how bad it seems.

Shortcut to Heaven

There is a shortcut to Heaven. The shortcut to heaven is to see yourself as blessed. For you are blessed. Everything you experience is a blessing in a bigger picture and serves the purpose of you knowing your true Self.

Every experience brings you closer to the realization of who you truly are, and that is the whole purpose and goal in life.

Every experience serves that one purpose. We don't learn from blessings as much as we do from suffering. That is due to the fact that when things go right and we are happy, we don't seek a deeper meaning to life. We are content with just accepting things as they are and never strive for an even better life.

Suffering however is not a necessity. If you already knew your true Self you would not experience nor have a need to experience suffering as you would already be at the goal and experience bliss.

The shortcut to heaven is to be and feel blessed now. Don't wait for things to happen or come to pass.

In this very moment you are creating what you will be experiencing in the future. Choose now, don't wait any longer. Life is awaiting you.

Being blessed and having blessings is a choice. Choose well.

About the Author:

Vivian Amis is the Author of "The Essentials of Life" and two children's books: "The Light Within You" and "One Big Shine".

Vivian is the author of many articles and quotes on spirituality/self-help. Her articles have appeared in Spiritual now, Wholistic Healing Research, Ezine Articles, New Times Naturally, Natural Awakenings, Expressions of the Soul, Spiritual Living 360 and Transformation. She lives with her husband, four children and two grandchildren in Tampa, Florida.

Other Books
by
Vivian Elisabeth Amis

From
I-nspire Direct Publications

The Essentials of Life

Reflections

Juvenile: One Big Shine

Juvenile: The Light Within You

38350340R00054

Made in the USA ·
Charleston, SC
07 February 2015